football's new wave

Peyton
Manning

Rising Son

BY
MARK STEWART

THE MILLBROOK PRESS
BROOKFIELD, CONNECTICUT

M

THE MILLBROOK PRESS

Produced by
BITTERSWEET PUBLISHING
John Sammis, President
and
TEAM STEWART, INC.

Series Design and Electronic Page Makeup by
JAFFE ENTERPRISES
Ron Jaffe

Researched and Edited by Mike Kennedy

All photos courtesy
AP/ Wide World Photos, Inc.
except the following:
SportsChrome, Michael Zito — Cover
University of Mississippi — Page 9
University of Tennessee — Page 11, 13, 14, 15, 19, 22 bottom, 24
The following images are from the collection of Team Stewart:
Sports Illustrated 8/26/96 © 1996 Time Inc.— Page 21
JBC © 1990 — Page 38
The Topps Co. © 1998 — Page 41 top
TCG © 1972 — Page 41 bottom
Pey Dirt, Inc. © 1999 — Page 44

Printed in the United States of America

Published by
The Millbrook Press, Inc.
2 Old New Milford Road
Brookfield, Connecticut   06804

Visit us at our Web site – http://www.millbrookpress.com

Library of Congress Cataloging-in-Publication Data

Stewart, Mark.
    Peyton Manning: rising son / by Mark Stewart
    p.   cm.   — (Football's new wave)
    Includes index.
    Summary: A biography of the Indianapolis Colts quarterback whose father was also a
professional quarterback.
    ISBN 0-7613-1517-9 (lib. bdg.)   — ISBN 0-7613-1332-X (pbk.)
    1. Manning, Peyton — Juvenile literature. 2. Football players—United States—Biography—
Juvenile literature. [1. Manning, Peyton. 2. Football players.] I. Title. II. Series.
GV939.M289S84 2000
796.332′092--dc21
[B]   99-35043
                                                                                            CIP

pbk: 1 3 5 7 9 10 8 6 4 2
lib: 1 3 5 7 9 10 8 6 4 2

Contents

Destined for Greatness

"Football got into our life early."
— PEYTON MANNING

The "American Dream" means different things to different people. To some, it means being rewarded for working hard and making a better life for your family. To others, it means becoming rich and famous, and enjoying luxuries most of us can hardly imagine. For Archie Manning, the dream was more like a fairy tale. He wanted to be an All-American quarterback, marry the homecoming queen, make a lot of money, and raise children who could elevate the family name to even greater heights.

Amazingly, that is exactly what Archie did. In 1970, while playing for the University of Mississippi, he was voted the top quarterback in the country. After graduation, he signed a lucrative NFL contract, married Homecoming Queen Olivia Williams, and between 1974 and 1979 had three strapping sons named Cooper, Peyton, and Eli.

The rest of the dream was up to the Manning kids. Archie and Olivia did not force their sons into football, but when your dad is a pro quarterback and you get to hang around football stadiums on the weekends, it can be a hard sport to resist. Not surprisingly, Cooper and Peyton were heaving footballs through the air as soon as they could stand. "They have tape of me when I was three years old," laughs Peyton, who claims you can hear his father shouting, "Do your drop-back, Peyton, do your drop-back!"

When the Indianapolis Colts made Peyton Manning the first pick in the 1998 NFL draft, it marked the beginning of a second generation of Mannings in professional football.

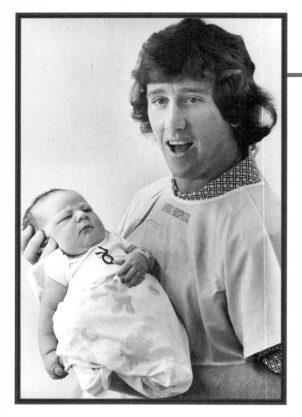

Archie Manning celebrates the birth of his first child, Cooper, in March of 1974.

The Mannings lived in a beautiful old home in the historic Garden District of New Orleans, Louisiana. Archie was the quarterback for the New Orleans Saints. He would work out during the week and play each Sunday—sometimes at home, sometimes on the road. Peyton and Cooper would wait impatiently for him to return from practice each afternoon so he could organize a pickup game with the kids who lived in the area.

Archie did not care if his sons played, he just liked to be with them. Football, he swears, was their choice. Peyton backs him up on this point. "Dad always wanted to spend time with us," he remembers. "We were the ones who always wanted to play football."

During the neighborhood games, Archie would either referee or serve as quarterback for both teams. Occasionally, he would stroll the sideline with a big video camera and film the action, announcing the game as if he were on television. Then the family would watch the tape and laugh. Peyton looks back on these days with great fondness. Life could not have been better. He had everything a boy could want, and there was no pressure to do anything other than have fun. Peyton's father looks back and realizes how important his "toy camera" turned out to be. After his playing days, he actually became a sportscaster. And Peyton developed a remarkable eye for detail from watching himself over and over again. In a way, Archie's home videos prepared them *both* for the future.

Did You Know?

Peyton did not play organized football until he was 13. "My school did not offer contact football until seventh grade," he says. "The younger leagues that offered it were not very organized, and my parents didn't think it would be a good experience."

In 1982, when Peyton was six, life got a little less fun. His dad was traded to the Houston Oilers. Archie and Olivia decided the family would stay in Louisiana. He would try to get back as much as he could during the season.

Sometimes the boys did not see their father for a week or more. Once in a while, though, Archie would surprise his sons and fly home for dinner. Then he would put them to bed and hustle back to the airport for the late flight back to Houston. The following season found Archie in Minnesota, playing for the Vikings. Minneapolis was too far away for surprise visits. Peyton, Cooper, and Eli really missed their dad. After one more season, he retired and came home.

Archie loved being back. His new career as a sportscaster was going well. He did not have to worry about being sandwiched by 350-pound (159-kg) defensive linemen anymore. And he finally had the time to watch his sons grow up. The first thing Archie noticed was how combative his two oldest boys were. Though two years younger than Cooper, Peyton was almost as strong and just as fast. He was also incredibly competitive. During pickup games, Cooper and Peyton would almost always end up on opposing sides, and they seemed to delight in pounding each other. They often emerged from these contests bloody and crying, and usually took their battles back home, where fights were likely to erupt at any time.

When Peyton reached seventh grade, he joined the Isidore Newman School's football team. His parents hoped that playing organized ball for the first time would dull his rivalry with Cooper. Instead, it became even more intense. Regardless of the game the Manning boys were playing, it almost always deteriorated into a personal war. And it was Archie's job to separate them. When he retired, he must have thought that his days of getting crunched by young football players were over. Now, instead of getting roughed up once a week, he was getting creamed practically every day!

"The day you two can finish a game without a fight will be a great day in my life."
ARCHIE MANNING

Growing and Throwing

"If there's any better quarterback his age out there in the country, I'd like to see him."

— JIM MORA, NEW ORLEANS SAINTS
HEAD COACH

When Peyton was not slugging it out with his brother, his competitive fire was being stoked by his teachers at Isidore Newman. One of the top private schools in New Orleans, Newman challenged its students to achieve in the classroom before they ever set foot on the athletic field. Peyton worked hard and did well in most of his classes, bringing home report cards full of A's and B's. Occasionally, he encountered a difficult subject. In these instances he would study extra-hard, and he refused to go to bed until he was satisfied that his homework assignment had been done flawlessly.

During Peyton's sophomore year at Newman, he won the starting quarterback job for the varsity football team.

Did You Know?

Peyton played two other sports for Newman. He spent four years as a shortstop, making second-team All-State as a senior. He also played guard on the basketball team during his freshman and sophomore seasons.

His parents were delighted with this development—not because he was following in his father's footsteps, but because he finally had no *choice* but to work things out with his

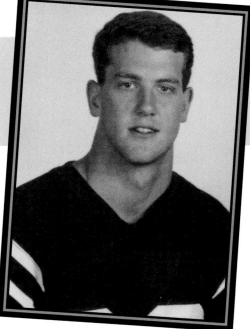

"He's all football. I like football, but Peyton lives to play football and be around it."
CHILDHOOD FRIEND WALKER JONES

older brother. Cooper, a senior, was the team's star pass receiver. If their sons could not learn to get along now, the entire school would suffer.

As the season's first game approached, everyone wondered whether they could pull it off. On Opening Day, the Mannings joined the entire student body in a great sigh of relief, as Peyton connected with his brother nine times in the first half. They continued to work together throughout the season, as Cooper caught 13 of Peyton's 23 touchdown passes. Newman went 12–2 and made it to the semifinals of the state playoffs.

Peyton was an enthusiastic learner. In school, he raised his hand a lot and asked his teachers lots of questions. At home, he was always asking his father how he could improve. Years earlier, Archie had promised Olivia that he would not "force-feed" football to his children. But Peyton was now hungry for information. The Mannings discussed their next move, and finally agreed that if their boy wanted to be a quarterback, he should get the full benefit of Archie's knowledge and experience. From that day on, there was a constant stream of information flowing from father to son. Over the next couple of years, Peyton absorbed more expert advice than most players receive in a lifetime.

Peyton also began building up his body, which was something that had never occurred to him before. "I did not lift weights until I was in eighth grade," Peyton remembers, adding that he really began to focus on his physique prior to his freshman year in high school—when he says he "really got serious about the fundamentals and the mechanics of the quarterback position." Archie, meanwhile, concentrated on the

"With what happened to Cooper, I've counted every day of football since my junior year in high school as lucky."

PEYTON MANNING

mental side of his son's game. He explained to Peyton that his attention to detail was a natural gift, and that he should develop it just like his throwing and footwork. He advised his son to watch videotapes of his games, and told him to ignore the ball and watch the entire field instead.

A good quarterback can "read" the defense by seeing how opposing players move in relationship to one another. If you can read the defense, then you can spot opportunities and also avoid big mistakes. Peyton spent hours reviewing films of his games during his junior year. As a result, he increased his passing yards and touchdowns, while cutting his interceptions by more than half.

As Peyton's senior year at Newman approached, he began to think of more ways to improve. Instead of watching grainy, low-quality videos from his own games, he began watching high-quality film from professional contests. At first, he was amazed at how different pro defenses were. But then he noticed they actually were doing the same things his high-school opponents were—only much better and much faster. As long as I can get better and faster, he thought, I might really be good enough to play in the NFL one day.

Peyton's senior year was simply spectacular. He threw for 2,703 yards and 39 touchdowns, and was honored as the country's High School Player of the Year. Big, strong, and smart, he could do it all—from attacking defenses for lightning-quick scores to working the clock on long drives. And he always kept his cool. Even when the team was behind and time was slipping away, Peyton could keep his teammates focused and execute the game plan. Newman's varsity coach, Tony Reginelli, said that Peyton ran the two-minute drill as well as anyone he had ever seen at any level.

Most of the college recruiters attending Peyton's games in the fall of 1993 agreed. They rated him as one of the best seniors they had ever evaluated. The Mannings were visited by a number of schools that wanted Peyton to play for them, and they faced some difficult decisions. Archie's school, Ole Miss, desperately needed a superstar, and put a lot of pressure on him to make Peyton go there. Archie and Olivia sat their son down and told him not to worry about what other people wanted him to do. They said go wherever you want. After careful consideration, Peyton narrowed his choices down to Michigan, Florida State, Notre Dame, Ole Miss, and Tennessee. In the end, he chose Tennessee.

Peyton waited until January 25, 1994, to announce his decision. And he held a press conference to reveal his choice. He had received so much publicity in high school that this was now a major news story. Every college football fan in the country was debating where he would go. Those rooting for him to follow in his father's footsteps and attend Ole Miss were disappointed. At the press conference, he apologized to the people of Mississippi, and asked them not to hold his choice against him.

Actually, Peyton had been planning to go to Ole Miss ever since Cooper received a scholarship to the school in 1992. The thought of teaming up with his brother and resurrecting the school's football program was very appealing to Peyton. But soon after Cooper joined the team, he was diagnosed with a rare disease called spinal stenosis.

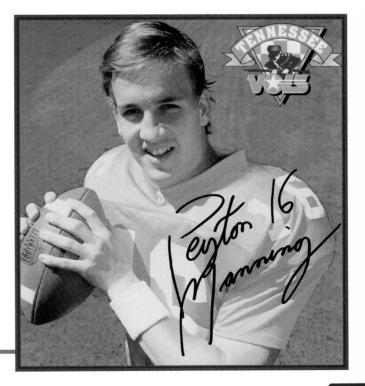

Doctors told him it was too dangerous to play football again. The news hit Peyton especially hard. He thought everything was all planned out. He wrote Cooper a letter imploring him to hang in there and stay positive. "I would like to live my dream of playing football through you," Cooper wrote back.

"I feel I'm playing for Cooper," says Peyton. "I can't imagine having football taken away. Now the game seems all the more precious to me."

Tennessee fans were ecstatic when Peyton announced he would join the "Vols."

Answering the Call

*"He came in with an attitude
I'd never seen before."*

— TENNESSEE TEAMMATE ERIC LANE

Peyton was one of two heavily recruited freshman quarterbacks to join the Volunteers in 1994. The other, Brandon Stewart, was also a gifted passer and play-caller. Peyton distinguished himself immediately, however, when he wandered onto the Tennessee campus six weeks before practice officially began and

asked if he could start working out with the team. It was not that he expected to win the starting job—upper classmen Jerry Colquitt and Todd Helton were way ahead of him—he just could not wait to start!

Head coach Phil Fulmer told Peyton that he probably would not see much action as a freshman, but that he had to

Did You Know?

Peyton took his schoolwork very seriously at Tennessee. Instead of taking the minimum number of courses, he took the maximum. He believed he might be ready to turn pro after three years, but did not want to leave college without a degree. By the end of his junior year, he had enough credits for a diploma.

work hard and pay attention to the starters. He expected him to be ready to compete for the number-one job as a sophomore. Peyton had every intention of developing into

Jerry Colquitt, the first-string quarterback at the start of Peyton's freshman year.

a starting quarterback, but he wanted to be ready sooner, just in case something happened and Coach Fulmer needed him to guide the team his freshman year.

Peyton's teammates were impressed by his talent, dedication, and ability to learn and execute. He also listened to what older players told him. Peyton knew there was no substitute for experience—if he could not get it from playing in actual games, he would try to get it from the guys who were playing. By the season opener, against UCLA, Peyton actually had a very good feel for the college game, even though he had never played a down.

Four minutes into the season opener, the unexpected occurred. Colquitt, the starter, went out with a severe injury and was lost for the season. Helton came in to replace him, but failed to move the offense. In desperation, Coach Fulmer put Peyton in the game. He played one series and handled himself well, then Helton went back in. Fulmer mostly wanted to see if Peyton had the confidence to fill in. He did. "It meant a lot to me," Peyton says of his coach's decision to play him.

Three weeks later, in a game at Mississippi State, Tennessee lost Helton, who went down with a bad knee. This time Peyton had to do more than just hand off. Coach Fulmer told the freshman that the game was his to win or lose. Peyton trotted on the field and called a play in the huddle. At the line of scrimmage, he barked out some signals, took the snap, and dropped back to pass. Peyton spotted an open man and rifled the ball to him for a 76-yard touchdown. He finished the game completing 14 of 23 passes—including a second touchdown—but Tennessee still lost by a field goal.

The following week, the Volunteers faced the unpleasant task of trying to salvage their season against the 17th-ranked Washington State Cougars. Coach Fulmer's record stood at one win and three losses, and he was going into battle without his two best quarterbacks. Peyton's performance against Mississippi State had been inspiring, but it came against a so-so team that had prepared to play against Helton. The Huskies, on the other hand, had an entire week to study films of Peyton. Also, their defense had not given up a touchdown all year.

To make matters worse, it was Homecoming Day on the Nashville campus. That meant thousands of the school's wealthiest and most influential alumni would be there

The fans at UT's Neyland Stadium take their football seriously. They were thrilled when Peyton came through after season-ending injuries to the starters.

for the game. If the Volunteers got slaughtered, it might cost millions of dollars in potential donations to the university. Peyton understood what was at stake. And if he had any questions about how much pressure the football program was under, they were answered by the coaching staff's pregame instructions: "Avoid losing."

Peyton had never gone onto a football field thinking this way. And he was not about to start. He knew his job against Washington State was to limit his mistakes, but he was looking to *win*. Coach Fulmer had developed an extremely conservative game plan, hoping to control the football for long periods of time and thus keep the scoring down. Peyton looked comfortable, played well, and recorded the first touchdown against the Huskies that season. The Volunteers' defense,

Did You Know?

To improve his foot speed, Peyton trained with weighted shoes. Once he had mastered the footwork of his position with a couple of pounds on each foot, he would take the weights off and be even quicker.

meanwhile, came up with enough big plays to limit Washington State to just one score. As Coach Fulmer had hoped, the contest developed into a tough defensive battle.

With the game tied 7–7 in the second half, the crowd really got into it and started making a tremendous amount of noise. Feeling the momentum build, the Tennessee coaching staff shifted its strategy. They believed the growing intensity of the game would eventually cause the Washington State defense to make a mistake. They told Peyton to keep his eyes peeled and strike quickly if he saw an opening. In the fourth quarter, he spotted a break-

"He's further along than any college quarterback I've seen in years. Maybe ever."

ALL-TIME GREAT COACH BILL WALSH

down in the coverage on receiver Kendrick Jones and whipped the ball to him for a 41-yard gain. John Becksvoort followed with a field goal to put Tennessee ahead 10–7, and the Volunteers held on for an incredible victory.

Peyton went on to turn the season around for Tennessee, directing the team to six wins in the next seven games. His best effort came against South Carolina, during which he threw for three touchdowns. Peyton was also at the helm in the Gator Bowl, when the Volunteers swamped Virginia Tech 45–23. For his remarkable freshman performance, Peyton was named Southeastern Conference Newcomer of the Year.

With no receivers in sight, Peyton prepares to make a dash for the end zone. His poise under pressure made him the SEC's top freshman in 1994.

Large and In Charge

"I think experience is your best teacher, and I got a lot of experience in college."

— PEYTON MANNING

Peyton's sophomore season began much differently than his freshman year. There was no longer any question regarding the team's number one starter. Jerry Colquitt's knee injury ended his career and Todd Helton decided to leave school and devote himself to baseball. Helton later became a star first baseman for the Colorado Rockies. Knowing he would be the starter, Peyton began working toward 1995 as soon as the 1994 season ended. Throughout the winter and spring, he watched endless hours of videotape, hoping to spot ways to improve his performance. Determined to eliminate mistakes, he reviewed the few bad plays he made as a fresh-

Did You Know?

During his junior year at Tennessee, Peyton sought the advice of many top athletes on whether or not he should turn pro. Among those he contacted were Tim Duncan, Michael Jordan, Fran Tarkenton, Roger Staubach, Phil Simms, Troy Aikman, and Drew Bledsoe. Most of the stars he polled told him to skip his last college season and enter the NFL draft.

man over and over. In the summer, Peyton organized unofficial practices with the team's key offensive players.

The Volunteers whipped through their 1995 schedule, as Peyton dismantled one opponent after another. He was the most sophisticated offensive player in college football, seeing and understanding things on the field that other quarterbacks did not. During preparation for upcoming games, Tennessee's coaches had to work late into the night just to keep up with the questions they knew Peyton would ask the next day. And when game time arrived, there was not a more confident and poised leader in the college ranks. Peyton threw for nearly 3,000 yards in 1995, and tossed 22 touchdown passes. He threw for 384 yards and four TDs against Arkansas, and 301 yards and three TDs against Alabama.

Two-sport star Todd Helton traded his helmet and shoulder pads for a bat and glove in 1995.

The season's only low point came against the University of Florida. The annual Tennessee-Florida game is one of the biggest grudge matches in college football. For a while, it looked as if things were under control, as Peyton guided the team to a 30–14 halftime lead. But in the second half, the Volunteers' defense collapsed and allowed 48

Peyton basks in the glory of victory after his 20-14 defeat of Ohio State in the 1996 Citrus Bowl.

points. The resulting 62–37 blowout haunted Tennessee all year, and ultimately prevented them from winning the national championship. After the season's final game—a 20–14 win over Ohio State in the Citrus Bowl—the Volunteers failed to achieve the number one ranking and had to settle for number two.

The Volunteers had another excellent season in 1996, and Peyton topped 3,000 passing yards. Once again, however, the year was marred by an embarrassing loss to Florida. Peyton played badly in the first half, throwing four interceptions, which let the Gators build a 35–0 lead. Peyton came charging back in the second half, and nearly pulled off the comeback of the year. He finished the day with 492 passing yards and four touchdowns. Unfortunately, it was too little, too late—Florida held on to win 35–29.

Peyton "lost" to Florida again after the season, when Gator quarterback Danny Wuerffel beat him out for the Davey O'Brien Award, which honors the nation's best college passer. Though he was told in advance he would not win, Peyton decided to attend the award banquet anyway. He knew many past winners would be there, and

AUGUST 26, 1996
$3.50 (CAN. $3.95)

Sports Illustrated

College Football '96

IN HIS FATHER'S IMAGE: PEYTON MANNING IDOL OF NO. 1 TENNESSEE

Sports Illustrated

SEPTEMBER 14, 1970   60 CENTS

TOP 20 IN COLLEGE FOOTBALL

Archie Manning Idol of Ole Miss

In 1996, Peyton and Archie became the first father-son football players to appear on the cover of SPORTS ILLUSTRATED.

Peyton and Kentucky quarterback Tim Couch meet after a 1996 game.

thought he would ask them if they believed he was good enough to skip his final season at Tennessee and go directly to the pros. Some watching him work the banquet said Peyton looked like a cop interrogating suspects. "I figured I had two hours with those guys," he laughs. "I wasn't going to waste it by making small talk!"

Peyton knew that he would be drafted in the first round if he left Tennessee early, but questioned whether he was really ready to go pro after three college seasons. Some scouts had whispered to him that he might be the first player taken. The New York Jets owned the top pick in the 1997 draft and were anxious to find a new signal-caller. The prospect of being a starting NFL quarterback in New York was both exciting and terrifying to Peyton. He needed a lot more information about the league before he decided whether to stay or go.

"You'd think he was a walk-on trying to prove something. He's really a driven young man."
JOHN STUCKY, TENNESSEE
STRENGTH AND CONDITIONING COACH

Not Enough Memories

chapter 5

"When Peyton made his announcement, I felt the earth shake."

— TENNESSEE HEAD COACH PHIL FULMER

T he National Football League knew all it needed to about Peyton Manning. Most coaches thought he was good enough to step right in and run a pro offense. Peyton was big and strong enough to withstand the punishment a rookie quarterback must endure. He was experienced and intelligent enough to adjust and improve each week.

Peyton also had one of the survival skills a pro quarterback needs most: a quick release. Indeed, he could read defenses so well, and drop back so fast, that he could launch an accurate throw before pass rushers ever got near him. Even in the face of an all-out blitz, Peyton usually had time to make a play.

Did You Know?

In his senior year, Peyton actually took on extra academic projects. "I really appreciate a student like him," says Tennessee professor Andy Kozar. "I told him, 'You really ought to consider getting a Ph.D. and being a professor.'"

"Peyton's the first to tell you he doesn't do it all himself."

UT COACH PHIL FULMER

Peyton was certain he would be successful in the NFL. But why, he wondered, did he have to start his pro career so soon? He liked college. He liked getting up early and lifting weights. He liked going to class and challenging his mind with subjects such as calculus and English literature. In the afternoons, the team would practice; in the evenings he would hit the books, alternating between his classwork and the Tennessee play manual.

To some, this may have seemed like an endless grind. But Peyton adored it. It felt good to walk around campus and have other students wish him good luck in his next game. And was there anything better than meeting his parents in the parking lot after games, having a little tailgate party, and then going out to dinner? Peyton knew he would never live this kind of life again.

He decided to stay. "I didn't have enough memories," he says. "If I had left early for the NFL, I wouldn't have had enough time to make as many friends away from football."

The sports world seemed shocked.

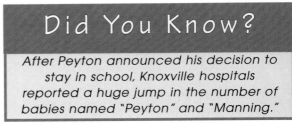

Did You Know?

After Peyton announced his decision to stay in school, Knoxville hospitals reported a huge jump in the number of babies named "Peyton" and "Manning."

Almost everyone thought Peyton would leave for the pros. Some believed he stayed so he could win the Heisman Trophy as the nation's top player. Peyton denies it. Others said he wanted one more crack at Florida, which had beaten Tennessee three times while Peyton was a Volunteer. This he does not deny. The winner of the 1997 Tennessee-Florida game would almost certainly win the SEC championship, and have a clear path to the national championship—the prize Peyton wanted most of all.

Tennessee began the season with a couple of easy wins, then began gearing up for the big Florida showdown. In the days leading up to the game, Florida coach Steve Spurrier and his players criticized Peyton and his teammates. They said he was overrated and that they knew just how to beat him. The Tennessee players knew exactly

Coaches
Corner

Here is what the people watching from the sidelines have said about Peyton over the years...

"You can talk about Peyton for hours, and it sounds like some fairy tale."
TENNESSEE HEAD COACH PHIL FULMER

"He has outstanding skills as a passer, he's fundamentally sound, and he seems mature beyond his years."
DAVID CUTLIFFE, UNIVERSITY OF TENNESSEE OFFENSIVE COORDINATOR

"There is no question that Peyton knows where to throw the football and when to throw the football."
MISSISSIPPI STATE HEAD COACH JACKIE SHERRILL

"I think he's phenomenal. He makes every throw. His mechanics are second to none."
GARY KUBIAK, DENVER BRONCOS' ASSISTANT

"He wants to do the best he can, and he wants you to give him all that you have to give him."
COLTS' HEAD COACH JIM MORA

Peyton's disappointment is clear as he congratulates Thaddeus Bullard after the 33–20 loss to Florida in 1997.

what Florida would try to do: The Gator defense would throw everything it had at Peyton and hope someone missed a blocking assignment or ran a bad pass route. The Volunteers practiced hard to make sure this did not happen.

Unfortunately for Peyton, the Gators made good on their boasts. Sending fresh linemen into the game on almost every play, Florida was able to penetrate Tennessee's pass blocking again and again. Poor Peyton spent the whole game dodging tacklers. Finally, the Gators forced the mistake they had been hoping for, as Peyton threw an interception. Florida defensive back Tony George plucked the ball out of the air and ran the length of the field for an 89-yard touchdown. Behind 14–0, the Volunteers were forced to abandon their running attack and throw the ball more often. Peyton, under constant pressure all day, played brilliantly the rest of the way. But Tennessee could never close the gap, and lost by 13 points.

A few days later, Peyton called a players-only meeting. He told his teammates that they still had a chance to win the national championship. It was still early in the season, and the teams ahead

The 1997 UT-Kentucky game was Peyton's greatest. He threw for 523 yards in a 59–31 blowout of the Wildcats.

of them in the rankings were not unbeatable. Yes, their fate now rested in the hands of others, but they would have no chance to reach number one if they did not pull together and play great football the rest of the way.

As it turned out, Peyton was right. Florida lost two games and dropped out of contention for the SEC and NCAA titles. Meanwhile, the Volunteers played great football and rolled over their remaining opponents. Peyton had a 523-yard passing day against Kentucky, and accounted for five touchdowns against Southern Mississippi. Against Alabama, he threw for 304 yards and three TDs. Afterward, Peyton was given the ultimate honor for a University of Tennessee student when he was selected to conduct the

Peyton conducts the school band in a rousing rendition of "Rocky Top" after winning the 1997 SEC championship.

Pride of Southland Band's rendition of "Rocky Top," the school song.

In the SEC championship game, Tennessee took on Auburn in the Louisiana Superdome, just a few miles from where Peyton grew up. He was supremely confident before the game, as were his teammates. Even when Auburn opened up a 20–7 lead, the Volunteers remained calm and took their cues from Peyton, who was focused and unflappable. He ended up leading Tennessee to a dramatic 30–29 win, and was honored as the game's MVP. "I knew we would win the game," Peyton says. "If we stayed calm, I knew we would win the game."

Wrapping Things Up

chapter 6

"Anyone who knows anything about me knows I did not come back to win individual awards."

— PEYTON MANNING

Although Peyton had established himself as the most highly regarded player in the nation, the conclusion of his college career was marked by sadness and disappointment. In November, Cooper was rushed to the hospital; his condition had deteriorated suddenly, and doctors needed to perform a delicate operation to keep him from getting any worse. Peyton could think of little else that winter, and admits that Cooper was on his mind during much of the Auburn game.

During that heroic effort, Peyton had smashed one of his knees on the artificial turf, and his leg swelled badly. As the Volunteers prepared to play in the Orange Bowl, he spent more time on the training table than on the practice field. Peyton's final game would be played against Nebraska, the country's number two team. Tennessee, ranked third, still had a chance at the national championship. If he beat Nebraska, and if top-ranked Michigan lost to Washington State in the Rose Bowl, then the Volunteers would

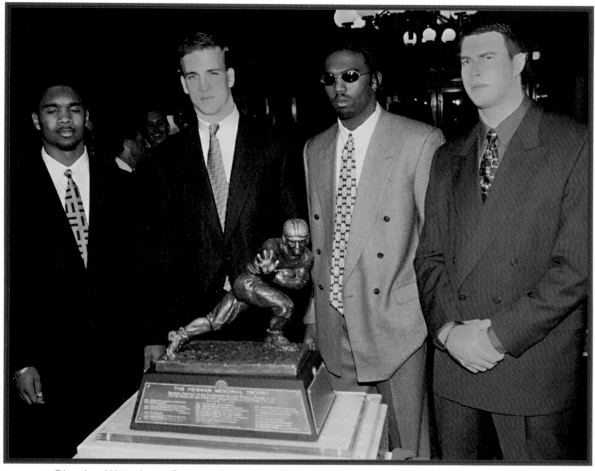

Charles Woodson, Peyton Manning, Randy Moss, and Ryan Leaf pose next to the Heisman Trophy prior to the 1997 award ceremony. Woodson was the surprise winner, with Peyton finishing second.

finish first. It was not a "long shot," either—Washington State, led by a dynamic young quarterback named Ryan Leaf, definitely had a chance to win.

Prior to the Orange Bowl, Peyton flew to New York to attend the Heisman Trophy ceremony. He had finished high in the voting in 1995 and 1996, and began 1997 as the favorite to win the award. When the winner was announced, it was Michigan defensive back Charles Woodson who was the top choice. Peyton was runner-up.

Finishing second in the Heisman Trophy voting was disappointing. But it was nothing compared to finishing second in the Orange Bowl, which is what happened on New

Year's Day. Peyton was still limping as the game approached, and Coach Fulmer knew that Nebraska would try to pressure his quarterback, just as Florida had. Fulmer reworked the game plan so that all Peyton had to do was deliver hand-offs and toss quick, short passes. Though he avoided the Cornhuskers' pass rush, Peyton could not move the Tennessee offense, throwing for just 134 yards. Nebraska, meanwhile, tore through the Volunteers for six touchdowns. The final score was 42–17. It was the most disappointing game of Peyton's life. And a lousy way to finish his college career.

Did You Know?

Peyton graduated from Tennessee cum laude, with a bachelor's degree in speech communication. He also minored in business and finished school with a 3.61 (A-) average. After his NFL career, Peyton plans to earn a master's degree in sports management.

college *stats*

Year	Attempts	Completions	Yards	TD Passes
1994	144	89	1,141	11
1995	380	244	2,954	22
1996	380	243	3,287	20
1997	477	287	3,819	36
TOTAL	**1,381**	**863**	**11,201**	**89**

college *highlights*

Sullivan Award (Top Amateur Athlete) 1997
Maxwell Award (NCAA Player of the Year) 1997
Davey O'Brien Award (Top College QB) 1997
All-American 1997
SEC Player of the Year .1997
MVP of SEC Championship Game 1997
Heisman Trophy Finalist 1995–1997
Academic All-American 1996–1997
First Team All-SEC . . . . .1995 & 1997
Second Team All-SEC .1996
SEC Newcomer of the Year 1994

Signing *Star*

Peyton is an autograph seeker's dream. He loves to chat with fans while scribbling his name and uniform number on scraps of paper. He remembers watching his father do the same. "I never forgot that," Peyton says. "I told myself that if I grew up and somebody wanted an autograph from me, I'd sign."

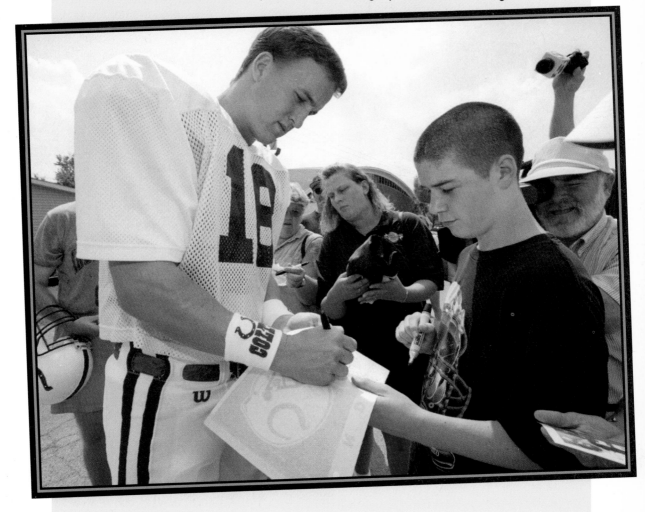

Leaf & Manning, Manning & Leaf

chapter 7

"It's like trying to figure out which is better, vanilla or chocolate."

— COLTS' GM BILL POLIAN

T he first selection in the 1998 NFL draft belonged to the Indianapolis Colts. The next pick was owned by the San Diego Chargers. Each team needed a quarterback with the ability to step in right away and learn "on the job." As luck would have it, the draft featured Peyton Manning and Ryan Leaf—a couple of guys who appeared to fit this description perfectly. For nearly four months in 1998, a great debate raged over who would make the better pro passer, and who would be drafted first.

"Peyton is a franchise quarterback."
COLTS' OWNER JIM IRSAY

Peyton stayed busy prior to the 1998 NFL draft. On a visit to the Tennessee capitol building, he met and signed an autograph for House Speaker Jimmy Nalfeh (above).

Most everyone agreed that Peyton would adjust to life in the NFL immediately, while some believed that Leaf needed to do a little more growing up before running a pro offense. Leaf had the stronger arm, Peyton more poise under pressure.

Peyton finally nosed ahead of Leaf when he worked out privately for a number of teams in March. The knock on Peyton was that he lacked the arm strength to be an

Peyton is flanked by Indianapolis owner Jim Irsay and NFL Commissioner Paul Tagliabue at the 1998 NFL draft. The Colts, who owned the first pick, already had a Manning #18 jersey ready to go.

All-Pro passer. In these exhibitions, however, he converted all nonbelievers by firing 20- and 30-yard spirals with great velocity and accuracy. Making these throws is the key to the pro passing attack.

On April 18 the Colts took Peyton with the first pick. Standing at the draft with Archie—who was the NFL's number two pick back in 1971—was one of the proudest

Peyton is all smiles after signing the richest contract for a rookie in NFL history.

> "We're putting him in there right away. We didn't draft this guy number one to sit on the bench."
> COLTS' HEAD COACH JIM MORA

moments of Peyton's life. "It's an exciting day," says Peyton of the draft. "You're starting one career and saying good-bye to another."

Less than a week after the draft, Peyton was in mini-camp, whipping balls to receivers and devouring the team's playbook. In three days of scrimmages, he made just one bad throw, and later practiced that same throw 35 times before he hit the showers. When training camp officially started, however, Peyton was nowhere to be found. Negotiations between his agent and the Colts had bogged down—the two sides agreed on the basics of the deal, but ironing out the details took far longer than anyone expected. By the time Peyton signed on the dotted line, he had missed eight practices, which is an eternity for an NFL rookie. Head coach Jim Mora threw Peyton right into the action, making him the starter in a full-contact scrimmage against the St. Louis Rams just three days after he reported to preseason camp.

Peyton played very well. While waiting to report to the Colts, he had memorized the playbook and viewed endless hours of videotape. Against St. Louis, he kept his cool under pressure and looked

Fullback Zack Crockett, one of the many talented young players Peyton joined when he signed with the Colts.

right at home on the field. Coach Mora, who had expected Peyton to be nervous and make mistakes, knew then that he had a very special player on his hands.

Mora was also feeling good about the rest of the team. Although the Colts had the NFL's worst record in 1997, they were not the league's worst club. Going into the season, they boasted a group of young stars, especially at the skill positions. Zack Crockett, a slashing runner with terrific blocking skills, was one of the top fullbacks in the American Football Conference. Marshall Faulk, his backfield mate, had lost a bit of speed after four pro seasons, but had become a great pass-catcher. Wide receiver Marvin Harrison and tight end Ken Dilger were smart route-runners with good hands.

The plan was for Peyton and his teammates to "grow up" together in 1998 and 1999, so Coach Mora and General Manager Bill Polian could see where they needed to bring in impact players. By the 2000 season, they expected Peyton to be the top passer in the division and the Colts to be contending for the AFC title.

The Peyton File

PEYTON'S FAVORITE...

Nickname . . . . "Caveman"
His pals in college gave it to him because he was so busy watching game films that he never came out of his dorm room.

Off-Field Job . . . . . . Public speaking

Fantasy . . . . Playing college ball in the 1960s

Philosophy . . . . . "Jimmy Connors said that he hated losing more than he loved winning. That's me!"

Country Singer . . . . . Kenny Chesney

Author . . . . Anne Rice
She was a neighbor when he was growing up.

Rock Singer . . . . Trent Reznor of Nine Inch Nails. He was also a neighbor in New Orleans.

Mammal . . . . Manning, the baby giraffe the Knoxville Zoological Gardens named after him

Peyton's dad is his role model.
"If I could play as long as my father did in the NFL—and also handle things the way he handled them—that would be a real achievement for me."

Baby Steps

chapter 8

"You can tell the guy's going to be a great quarterback."

— MIAMI STAR TRACE ARMSTRONG

eyton made his professional debut against the Miami Dolphins in the season's opening game. Much was made of the fact that he would begin his NFL career against the great Dan Marino. Some said this game was a symbolic "passing of the torch." But knowledgeable fans understood that it would be a while before Peyton was ready to compare himself to Marino. Besides, he was more like Troy Aikman of the Cowboys. Like

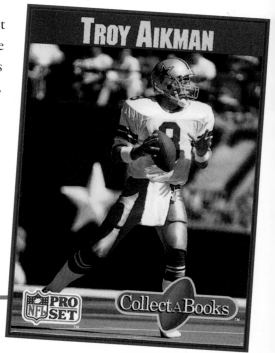

Dallas quarterback Troy Aikman "wrote the book" on precision passing in the 1990s. Peyton is often compared to the Cowboys' superstar.

Dan Marino congratulates Peyton after his first pro game. The Dolphins beat the Colts 24–15, despite Peyton's 302 passing yards.

Aikman, Peyton was an efficient passer who specialized in carefully probing opponents and then burning them for big plays the instant they let their defenses down.

As the contest unfolded, Peyton made some nice throws and kept the Colts in the game. But he made a rookie mistake near the end, challenging veteran defensive-back Terrell Buckley. Buckley intercepted Peyton's pass and ran it back for a touchdown to seal a Miami victory. Peyton finished his pro debut with a very respectable 21

Ryan Leaf offers his hand in congratulation to Peyton, who led the Colts to a 17-12 win over the Chargers in their first meeting.

completions and 302 passing yards. Over the next three weeks, he showed similar flashes of brilliance and made similar mistakes. As a matter of fact, he was leading the AFC in both passing yards and interceptions— an unusual combination. Unfortunately, the Colts lost each time.

In the season's fourth game, Indianapolis hosted San Diego. Ryan Leaf already had two wins under his belt, but he was off to a bumpy start with the Chargers. He had been booed by the San Diego fans, and reacted by criticizing them in the media. Despite an 0–4 record, Peyton was still on good terms with Indianapolis fans. When the final gun sounded on this "rookie showdown," the Colts were 17–12 winners, and Peyton was the most popular guy in town.

Peyton improved dramatically over the next four games, even though the Colts lost each one. The contests were close and well played, however. The 34–31 loss to the San Francisco 49ers, in fact, might have been the Colts' finest performance of the season. In an unfor-

Did You Know?

Peyton talks to his grandparents all the time during the season, and visits them in Mississippi during the off-season. Grandma Manning lives in Drew, while Olivia's parents live in the town of Philadelphia.

gettable shootout with Steve Young, Peyton completed 18 of 30 passes, had no interceptions, and threw for three touchdowns. The following week, in a five-point loss to

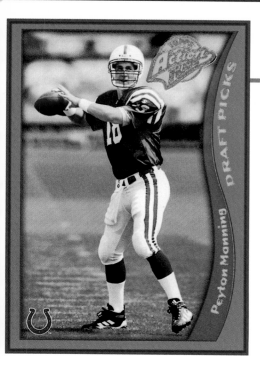

the Patriots, Peyton completed a season-high 30 passes. Peyton despised losing, but felt the Colts were on the verge of doing great things.

The Colts scored their second victory of the year against the toughest team in their division, the New York Jets. Peyton completed 26 passes and threw for three TDs as Indianapolis prevailed in a 24–23 thriller. The team's third and final win of the year came against the Cincinnati Bengals. Peyton was as sharp as he had been all season, leading the Colts to a 39–26 victory.

There is no such thing as a "great" 3–13 season. Losing hurts, and failing to improve on the league's worst record is embarrassing. But the Colts closed the book on 1998 with smiles on their faces. The players had given everything they had, in every game, all season long. In 10 of their 13 defeats, they were within striking distance of their opponents in the fourth quarter. They had learned important lessons about winning and losing, and believed in their ability to improve in the coming years.

As for Peyton, he had turned in an awesome rookie performance. He established new league records for rookies with 3,739 passing yards and 26 touchdowns. His 326 completions set a new team record. More important to the Colts than records was that Peyton had developed into a confident team leader. On the field, he had become so good at reading defenses that he would often call two plays in the huddle, then choose which one he

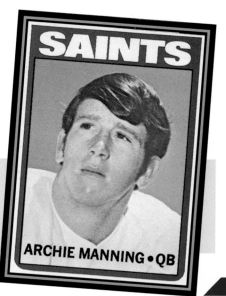

ARCHIE MANNING • QB

"Peyton is so much farther along than I was when I came into the league. He's ready for this challenge."
ARCHIE MANNING

wanted to run when he got to the line of scrimmage. Off the field, he invited the coaches to really "let him have it" if he did something wrong, so his teammates would see that he was not getting special treatment. And he never ducked the media, answering endless questions even after a painful loss.

The Colts, satisfied that they possessed the NFL's next great quarterback, set about the task of building a team that could grow quickly with Peyton. In the 1999 draft, they passed on a chance to get Heisman Trophy winner Ricky Williams and instead took Edgerrin James of the University of Miami. A terrific runner, James also has great hands, making him an ideal target for Peyton. Indianapolis added guard Brandon Burlsworth, an exceptional blocker who should be protecting Peyton for years to come. The Colts also got Hunter Smith, a punter from Notre Dame, and Florida linebacker Mike Peterson—one of the guys who drove Peyton crazy back when the Gators "owned" the Tennessee Volunteers.

Did You Know?

Peyton served as honorary grand marshall for the Louisiana Special Olympics in May of 1998. Since then he has set aside tens of thousands of dollars from Manning Passing Academy tuitions and donated the money to Special Olympics Louisiana.

Going into the 1999 season, the Colts were chosen by some to shoot right past the Patriots, Dolphins, Bills, and Jets, and challenge for the AFC's Eastern Division title. It shows the impact a good young quarterback can have on a team—not just on its offense, but on its defense, too. Thanks to Peyton, Indianapolis now ranks among the most exciting teams in all of football.

pro stats

Year	Attempts	Completions	Percentage	Yards	TD Passes
1998	575*	326**	56.7	3,739**	26

pro highlights

NFL All-Rookie First Team 1998
NFL Rookie Records . . . . . . .Attempts, Completions, Yards & TDs

*Led NFL   **Led AFC

Bobby Hamilton of the Jets is hot on Peyton's trail, as the Colts try to pull off an improbable comeback win. Indianapolis prevailed 24-23 for its second victory of the 1998 season.

Nice Work If You Can Get It

chapter 9

> *"It really doesn't matter what you do in college. It's what you do in the pros when you get there."*
>
> — PEYTON MANNING

There are no guarantees of success in the National Football League. Some of the greatest college quarterbacks never make it in the pros. Peyton knows how fortunate he is to have closed out his first season on a positive note. Ryan Leaf, his "twin" in the 1998 draft, lost his starting job in San Diego and was criticized for his impatience and lack of maturity. Most of the experts believe that Leaf will one day find success in the NFL, but his story is typical of young college stars thrust too soon into a starting job.

Rather than taking a well-earned rest, Peyton began thinking about the 1999

Peyton loves surfing the Internet, checking out both sports and non-sports Web sites. He often enters chat rooms and identifies himself as Peyton Manning. But, of course, no one believes him.

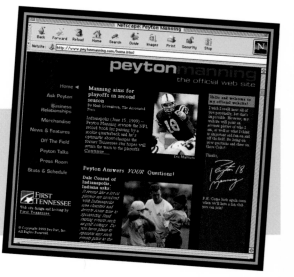

Peyton makes sure to set aside time to spend with his fans.
He believes it is part of a pro athlete's duties.

season as soon as the final gun sounded on the last game of the 1998 campaign. He knows he took the league a little by surprise, and that everyone will be gunning for him in the coming years. He recognizes that the line between success and failure in the NFL can be a fine one, and that there are hungry young players anxious to replace him if he ever takes his job for granted. Peyton also knows that the league itself is counting on him. As veteran quarterbacks such as John Elway, Dan Marino, Troy Aikman, and Steve Young fade from the scene, a new generation of passers will emerge. Right now, Peyton is the leading light among these young guns.

Being the NFL's "glamour boy" is both a blessing and a curse for Peyton. On the positive side, his team has a lot of money invested in him, which means they will pro-tect their investment by surrounding him with good players. On the negative side, he accepts the fact that, as an instantly recognizable public figure, part of his life belongs to the fans. Actually, Peyton admits he kind of likes all the public appearances and

Peyton stretches next to Edgerrin James (32), the Colts' top draft pick in 1999.

speech making he has to do. Also, in a weird way he feels that the constant scrutiny NFL stars must endure has its advantages. "I think it makes you a better person," Peyton explains. "You make the right decisions and hang around the right people because you know people are watching you."

The biggest hassle about being a celebrity is that he has little time left for himself. Right now, that is okay—Peyton is not married, and his commitments outside of football are few. He knows, however, that it will be hard to start a family and be there for his wife and kids. Of course, he knows it can be done. Archie did a heck of a job back when Peyton was growing up.

In the meantime, Peyton is busy getting used to life as an NFL quarterback, which can be pretty *un*glamorous. The excitement of his rookie year has faded away, and it is beginning to feel like a job. During the season, Peyton wakes up around 6:00 A.M. each morning and sits down to breakfast at the Colts' practice facility at 7:00. After watching some film or studying the playbook for a few minutes, the meetings begin. The Indianapolis coaches fill Peyton in on the team's next opponent—what they do well, what they don't do well, and what surprises they might be cooking up for him come Sunday afternoon. Before lunch, the team gathers on the field and walks through some of the new plays that will be used in the upcoming game. After lunch, Peyton goes back into meetings. There is more discussion, more analysis, and more film to watch.

Finally, the players get suited up for practice. Practice usually lasts two hours, during which Peyton goes through all of the running and passing plays with his teammates. If someone messes up, the coaches blow their whistles and scream, then make everyone line up and do it again until they get it right.

Around 4:00 P.M., practice ends. Some players go to the weight room, while others visit the trainer to tend to their aches and pains before leaving the complex. Peyton usually stays until after dark, attending more meetings and watching more film. "Friday's and Saturday's practices are not quite so long, so I'll get home earlier," he says. "But it's a full week."

Peyton also knows that being a pro quarterback involves shouldering the blame when the Colts do not play well. He is not anticipating any more 3-13 seasons, but recognizes that the growing process will include some tough losses. If the fans point their fingers at him, then so be it. "It's part of the job," Peyton says. "Just like lifting weights or going to meetings or throwing on your own."

Or *winning*. Which is something Peyton is expected to do a lot of. Indeed, over the next few seasons the pressure will be on him to do more than get the Colts into the end zone; he will be asked to lead the team to the next level. Indianapolis fans are confident he can do that, and more. So is Peyton. He has waited a long time for this chance, and he aims to make the most of it. Peyton is determined to make all of those extra hours in the film room, the weight room, and on the field pay off. And he is determined to have fun doing it.

Football may be a job, but it's a darn good one, and Peyton knows it. Win or lose, he plans to have the time of his life.

Peyton really enjoys public appearances. During the off-season he delivers dozens of inspirational speeches.

Index

PAGE NUMBERS IN ITALICS REFER TO ILLUSTRATIONS.